21ST CENTURY DEBATES

SURVEILLANCE

THE IMPACT ON OUR LIVES

SCARLETT MccGWIRE

RAINTREE
Steck-Vaughn
PUBLISHERS

A Harcourt Company

Austin   New York
www.steck-vaughn.com

21st Century Debates Series

Climate Change	Energy	Genetics
Internet	Media	Rain Forests
Surveillance	Waste and Recycling	

Published by Raintree Steck-Vaughn Publishers, an imprint of Steck-Vaughn Company

Library of Congress Cataloging-in-Publication Data
MccGwire, Scarlett.
Surveillance: the impact on our lives / Scarlett MccGwire.
    p.   cm.—(21st century debates)
    Includes bibliographical references and index.
    ISBN 0-7398-3174-7
    1. Surveillance—Juvenile literature.
    [1. Surveillance.]
    I. Title. II. Series.

Printed in Italy. Bound in the United States.
1 2 3 4 5 6 7 8 9 0 04 03 02 01 00

Picture acknowledgments: AFP/Corbis 11; Barclays 46; Bettmann/Corbis 10, 19; Boots Company plc 47; Cellnet 37; Corbis 5, 9 (The Purcell Team), 12 (Digital Art), 15 (Tim Wright), 27 (Steve Raymer), 28 (Roger Ressmeyer), 33 (Amos Nachoum), 36 (Kelly-Mooney Photography), 45 (Peter Turnley), 56 (Kit Kittle); Mary Evans Picture Library 4; Genesis Space Photo Library 13, 52, 53; The Ronald Grant Archive 8, 34, 40; HO/Official USMC/Reuters/Popperfoto 6; News International Syndication/Times Newspapers Ltd. 38 (Andy Watts); Norbain plc 30, 35; Panos Pictures 29 (Jeremy Horner); Popperfoto 18, 41; Popperfoto/Reuters 48; Quadrant Picture Library 58; Racal 44; Reuters Newsmedia Inc/Corbis 42; Reuters/Popperfoto 16; Science Photo Library 21 (James King-Holmes), 32 (Victor de Schwanberg), 51 (U.S. Geological Survey); Tony Stone Images 17 (Kevin R. Morris), 23 (David Joel), 24 (Roger Tully), 26 (Jim Krantz), 31 (Alan Thornton), 49 (Bob Schatz), 54 (Doug Armand), 55 (Dan Bosler), 59 (Don Spiro).

Cover: foreground picture shows a U.S. Airforce Lockheed spy plane (Quadrant Picture Library); background picture shows a colored radar satellite image of farmland used for mechanized agriculture in the Ukraine (NASA/Science Photo Library).

CONTENTS

THE DEVELOPMENT OF SURVEILLANCE

High-Tech Watching— A Good or Bad Thing?

An American magazine from the 1930s shows a private eye tailing a suspect.

Surveillance is the monitoring and documenting of various aspects of people's lives to find out when rules are being obeyed or broken. It has been with us for centuries. Governments have always employed spies to keep an eye on their enemies and sometimes even on their allies. The police have had people tailed (followed), and they have paid informers to tip them off about crimes that are being planned. Today, surveillance is carried out in person, or by using photographic, video, or audio techniques. New technology makes the tracking of people far easier than it used to be. Businesses use computer technology to gain useful information about their customers, remote-control cameras watch us as we walk down the street, and our telephone conversations and e-mails can be monitored. In the United States, e-mails are subject to intelligence scanning for key words at a rate of two million per hour.

When emperors, kings and queens, czars, or dictators governed countries, these rulers had absolute power. But when people began to elect their own governments, they started to question the authority of those who monitor the activities of other citizens. In modern society, technological surveillance serves a positive purpose: It is widely used to apprehend criminals, for example. But surveillance technology is also open to abuse, and many people are now asking questions about the nature and uses of surveillance.

This book examines the effect that technology has had on surveillance and its implications for our rights as citizens. How much do the government, the police, and business corporations know, and how much do they have a right to know? What laws, if any, are needed to protect us?

A slow process

Until the 1960s, most surveillance was low-tech and expensive. If you wanted to watch suspects, you had to tail them. To follow a person, at least six people, organized in teams of two, were required daily to work three eight-hour shifts. All the material and contacts gathered had to be typed up and filed away, which meant that cross-checking (for example, finding a red-headed man who had committed a robbery) took a long time. Even electronic surveillance, like phone tapping, was highly labor-intensive because the results had to be typed up. However, by the 1980s, new forms of electronic surveillance had emerged, many of which were aimed at making phone taps and other interceptions of communications automatic. Today, the development of computer technology has made cross-checking almost instantaneous.

Before the introduction of new technology, the checking of surveillance data was a laborious process. Here Federal Bureau of Investigation (FBI) staff check fingerprint files.

Surveillance technology consists of devices and systems that can monitor, track, and assess the movements of people and their property. In western democracies, this technology is used to track people suspected of being involved in organized crime, such as terrorism and drug running. It is also used by employers to track the behavior of their employees and by private investigators seeking evidence for their clients. However, it is also sometimes used to follow the activities of political dissidents, such as environmental activists and animal liberationists. Elsewhere surveillance is used to track people who are perceived to be a threat to the state; these may include human rights activists, journalists, student leaders, minorities, union leaders, and political opponents.

Businesses use surveillance extensively. In shopping malls, video cameras or closed circuit television (CCTV) cameras provide a record of customers' movements. The random monitoring of customer phone calls helps businesses gain a profile of their clients so that they can target their products more effectively.

A soldier tests out his night-vision goggles prior to a combat exercise in the dark in the Persian Gulf. This technology can also be used for surveillance purposes.

A growth industry

A huge range of surveillance technologies has evolved. Night-vision goggles allow spies to see in the dark. Parabolic microphones detect conversations over a mile away, and the laser version can pick up a conversation through a closed window. The Danish Jai stroboscopic camera can take hundreds of pictures in a matter of seconds and is capable of photographing every single participant in a demonstration or march. Automatic vehicle recognition systems track cars around a city by way of a system of maps. New technologies, originally developed for the defense and intelligence sectors during the Cold War between what used to be the Soviet Bloc and the West, have, since the collapse of communism, rapidly become available to the police and private companies.

The West has led the way in the development of surveillance technology. It has provided, and continues to provide, invaluable support to military and totalitarian regimes throughout the world. One British computer firm provided the technology for the South African automated Passbook, a means of identification used by the apartheid regime in that country to discriminate against nonwhite citizens. In the 1980s, an Israeli company developed and exported the technology for a computerized death list used by the Guatemalan police. Surveillance is an important activity in the pursuit of intelligence and political control by military and totalitarian regimes. Many countries in transition to democracy also rely heavily on surveillance to satisfy the demands of the police and the military.

New technology makes possible the mass surveillance of populations. In the past, regimes relied on targeted surveillance. With new technology, the financial transactions, communications activities, and geographic movements of millions of people can be tracked, analyzed, and transmitted cheaply and efficiently.

In 1948, George Orwell's novel *1984* was published. It was a terrible vision of a society in which the citizens were constantly under the surveillance of a dictator called Big Brother. Of course, we do not have televisions in our homes

FACT

An adult in the developed world is located, on average, on three hundred databases. Many people in the West are entangled in a web of surveillance that embraces everything from bank accounts to e-mail.

John Hurt as Winston Smith tries to evade the ever-watchful eye of Big Brother in the film version of George Orwell's novel 1984.

VIEWPOINT

"The telescreen received and transmitted simultaneously. Any sound that Winston made, above the level of a very low whisper, would be picked up by it; moreover, so long as he remained within the field of vision which the metal plaque commanded, he could be seen as well as heard. There was, of course, no way of knowing whether you were being watched at any given moment."
George Orwell, from his novel 1984

DEBATE

How do we balance our right to privacy with the government's need to know what we are doing so that we do not cause harm?

recording our every move. However, the amount of information that is known about each of us is considerable. In Orwell's 1984, government power was obvious and frightening. As real-life citizens at the dawn of a new millennium, we have no idea who is watching, listening, or keeping tabs on us. But if someone wants to, it is only too easy.

In most democracies there are laws that control the use of surveillance by state bodies. These laws usually fall into two groups: those controlling the act of surveillance, such as telephone tapping (including e-mails) and bugging devices; and those regulating the personal information that may be gained from surveillance. However, not all surveillance techniques are covered and, as we shall discover during the course of this book, serious questions still arise concerning the effectiveness of much surveillance legislation.

Clearly there are many good reasons for surveillance. It has not only resulted in the arrest of many criminals, but also prevented crimes from being committed. But, as we shall see, it is an increasingly powerful tool that can be abused.

GOVERNMENT SURVEILLANCE

Security Strategies or State Snooping?

What happens when a government abuses its power? In countries governed by totalitarian regimes, such as China, citizens know that they are under surveillance. But what happens when democratic governments carry out surveillance strategies that appear to contradict the meaning of the word democracy? As citizens, how do we know whether the state is protecting us or defending its own interests?

Government surveillance in the West uses advanced technology to provide the most sophisticated methods available. Billions of dollars are spent on developing state-of-the-art techniques that are later sold to commercial companies and developing countries.

Governments concentrate on gathering intelligence about foreign countries as well as keeping an eye on their own citizens. The secret interception of foreign communications has been practiced by almost every advanced nation since international telecommunications were invented. This communications intelligence, known as Comint, provides governments with information about foreign events. In the developed world, information is the key to maintaining power and influence.

> **FACT**
>
> Every year, about 15 to 20 billion dollars is spent on Comint, mostly by the United States, Canada, Great Britain, Australia, and New Zealand.

In China, citizens know that their actions may be scrutinized by the authorities.

The intelligence services use surveillance techniques to monitor the activities of organized criminals. Until recently these techniques were fairly basic. Here FBI agents stake out the house of Mafia boss Sam Giancana in 1963.

The most traditional Comint targets are military messages and diplomatic communications between national capitals and missions abroad. This means that, for example, the British intelligence service listens in on communications between the Chinese Embassy in London and Beijing. Since the 1960s, following the growth of world communications, the gathering of information about economic, scientific, and technical development has become increasingly important. More recent targets for intelligence gathering include drug traffickers, money launderers, terrorists, and organized criminals.

At home, the government uses the interception of telecommunications to spy on people it believes are a danger to the state. In democracies these tend to be organized gangs of criminals or terrorists. In dictatorships, human rights groups, reporters, and political opponents are the most common targets. In some countries, such as Honduras and Paraguay, the state-owned telecommunications companies actively help the security services monitor those fighting for human rights. Also, intelligence gathered for one purpose can be used for another. Between 1967 and 1975, the United States and British intelligence services used information from Comint that had been collected primarily for other purposes to provide data about political opposition figures.

Spy satellites

The United States has the most powerful network of spy satellites in the world. It can intercept communications signals anywhere on the planet. The United States is part of the USA/UK alliance, which includes the English-speaking countries of Australia, New Zealand, Canada, and Great Britain. This alliance uses the Echelon network of satellites.

FACT

In the United States from the mid-1940s until 1974, the Red Squad, comprising members of the Michigan State police, kept files on people suspected of being communists even though they had committed no crime. It was believed that such people posed a threat to the political system of the country.

Other spy satellites include Russia's FAPSI, which relays information via large collection sites at Lourdes in France, Cuba, and at Cam Ranh Bay, Vietnam; Germany's BND; and France's DGSE. The latter two are said to collaborate at a collection site at Kourou, Guyana, and are targeted on North and South American satellite communications.

Most people have no idea of the number of government satellites orbiting the Earth, taking pictures of us and listening in on our telephone conversations. These are secret operations. We may be photographed and have all our electronic communications intercepted without even being aware that somewhere in space a satellite is passing overhead.

However, some of these satellites are tracked by amateur watchers. The orbital paths and schedules of the five known U.S. spy satellites are posted on the Internet. Armed with a personal computer and a basic understanding of astronomy, it is now possible to calculate when the satellites will pass over any point on Earth.

FACT

Most democracies have laws that limit the powers of government surveillance. In the United States, for example, the National Security Agency is prohibited from deliberately eavesdropping on U.S. citizens unless it can establish probable cause to suggest that they are agents of a foreign government, committing espionage or other crimes.

In recent years surveillance technology has become ever more complex. Here Gerry Adams, leader of Sinn Fein, the political wing of the IRA, holds a bugging device he claims the British security services planted in his car.

An artist's impression of a satellite relaying signals to and from a receiving station.

FACT

Echelon has existed since the 1970s and was greatly enlarged between 1975 and 1995. In the mid-1980s, it began to make heavy use of the American and British global communications network. In 1991, a British television program reported that the system secretly intercepts every single telex passing through London. It picks up thousands of diplomatic, business, and personal messages every day.

Satellites work by picking up radio signals that pass directly into space. These signals are used to provide global communication and to intercept such communications in space and on land. Long distance microwave radio relay links may require dozens of intermediate stations to receive and re-transmit communications. Each subsequent receiving station picks up only a tiny fraction of the original signal, while the remainder passes over the horizon and on into space. This is known as microwave spillage. The best position for satellites to pick up on microwave spillage is not above the chosen target, but up to 80 degrees of longitude away. This technique was used during the 1960s to provide intelligence gathering from space.

Echelon

Echelon is an integrated global network of satellite and associated relays. It is the most powerful spy satellite network we know about. It is used to intercept ordinary e-mails, faxes, telexes, and telephone conversations throughout most of the world. It targets governments, organizations, businesses, and individuals, but it could affect almost anyone. The five security agencies that run Echelon are the United States National Security Agency (NSA), the New Zealand Government Communications Security Bureau (GCSB), the British Government Communications Headquarters (GCHQ), Canada's Communications Security Establishment (CSE), and the Defense Signals Directorate (DSD) in Australia.

Echelon is not designed to eavesdrop on a particular individual's e-mail or fax link. Instead, it intercepts very large quantities of communications and uses computers to identify and extract messages of interest from the mass of unwanted ones. A chain of secret interception facilities has been established around the world: some monitor communications satellites, others monitor land-based communications networks, and others monitor radio communications. Echelon links all these facilities together, providing the United States and its allies with the ability to intercept a large proportion of the communications on the planet.

An important point about the new system is that, before Echelon, different countries and different stations knew what was being intercepted and to whom it was being sent. Now a tiny proportion of the messages are read locally. The rest are sent straight to the National Security Agency in the United States, which means that the other allies are no longer being kept fully informed.

FACT

During the Cold War, the United States used spy satellites to record the activities of the Soviet Union and China. Scientists are now using some of these pictures to measure ecological changes such as global warming.

A Russian spy satellite photograph of the pyramids in Egypt. Satellites are used for taking photographs and intercepting communications.

VIEWPOINTS

Until recently, Echelon was a closely guarded secret. But some members of the New Zealand intelligence service became worried about the powerfulness of the system and feared that it was being abused by the countries running it, in particular the United States. In 1988, the British journalist Duncan Campbell revealed the existence of Echelon in an article in the *New Statesman* magazine. And in 1996, a book called *Secret Power* was published by New Zealand author Nicky Hagar, also revealing details of the Echelon system. In 1998 a British newspaper, *The Sunday Times*, discovered that the United States was using information from Echelon to help U.S. companies bid for contracts against competitors in other countries. The paper reported that the U.S.-run Menwith Hill interception station in North Yorkshire in Great Britain was monitoring information about business deals.

Inside information

Journalists have also shown that Echelon has benefited U.S. companies involved in arms deals because it has provided them with inside information. In 1990, the U.S. intercepted secret negotiations between Indonesia and Japan and persuaded Indonesia to include the huge U.S. company AT&T in a multibillion-dollar telecommunications deal that at one point was going solely to Japan's NEC. And in 1995, when the United States was in crucial World Trade Organization talks with Europe over a dispute with Japan over car part exports, Echelon provided information about the Japanese that strengthened the U.S. position.

It is alleged that the NSA has, through Echelon, intercepted conversations between the German company Volkswagen and General Motors. And the French have complained that their electronics company, Thompson CSF, lost a $1.4 million deal to supply Brazil with a radar system because the NSA intercepted details of the negotiations and passed them on to the U.S. company Raytheon, which subsequently won the contract. The European company, Airbus Industrie, believes it lost a $1 billion contract to the U.S. companies Boeing and McDonnell Douglas because of information intercepted by United States surveillance systems.

Reaction to the news of Echelon and, in particular, to the way it spied on European countries from the UK, was swift and critical. The leading Italian business magazine, *Il Mondo*, featured the issue as its cover story for two weeks in 1998. The following week, the French daily newspaper *Liberation* devoted its first four pages to the NSA under the headline "How the US Listens to the Planet." Other European countries quickly followed suit by questioning the right of the UK to play host to the United States in this way.

The American Sugar Grove Electronic Surveillance Center, photographed here in 1992, has become one of the NSA's top listening posts.

VIEWPOINTS

"Major governments are routinely utilizing communications intelligence to provide commercial advantage to companies and trade."
Duncan Campbell, British journalist

"The nation's spy satellites typically produce far too much information for overworked and under-trained intelligence analysts to handle."
U.S. retired admiral Daniel Jeremiah, in a classified report to the CIA, 1998

An artist's representation of the Helios spy satellite.

It is understandable that countries spy on each other to protect their citizens from outside threats. Intelligence gathered from surveillance might alert a country to the danger of falling behind a potential enemy in the arms race, or it could provide information that would allow a country to take evasive action to avoid conflict. But it is not so easy to justify commercial surveillance, as the European reaction to Echelon demonstrated.

So, does commercial surveillance provide any positive benefits to society, or does it simply benefit the nation that carries it out? If a secret spy system can see all the hands in the international business poker game, then it automatically places those in control of the system at a distinct advantage. The Echelon system is set up to maintain the status quo, which means that the existing inequalities in the global power struggle are reinforced.

It is not only commercial companies that have their communications intercepted. In the 1970s and 1980s, the British military intelligence center, GCHQ, spied on charities including Amnesty

International and Christian Aid by monitoring all their communications. But it should be remembered that most countries play dirty when they can. The French spy on the United States and on other western countries' telephone and cable traffic by way of the *Helios 1A* spy satellite.

However, western countries do not have a completely free hand in using their satellites. In theory, all the countries using Echelon have laws that govern the kind of interceptions that gather communications intelligence under this system.

Underwater cable interception

Cables laid under the sea take an enormous amount of international telecommunications traffic and, for a long time, were believed to be secure from interception. However, in 1971, an American submarine successfully tapped a cable off the coast of the former Soviet Union. The tap continued until 1982, when a NSA employee sold information to the Soviets about the operation, code-named "Ivy Bells." The part of the "Ivy Bells" that was used to make the recordings is now on display in the Moscow museum of the former KGB (Russia's secret police). The United States is still the only naval power known to have deployed deep-sea technology for that purpose, and it has greatly extended its cable-tapping operations in the last fifteen years. It appears that the richer countries of the world can buy the technology necessary to break any code or infiltrate any network. What impact might this have on society as a whole?

A U.S. Navy nuclear submarine surfacing off the coast of Alaska. The United States is the only naval power known to have used deep-sea technology for cable-tapping.

FACT

During the mid-1980s, French counter-intelligence agents tapped the telephones of prominent journalists and political leaders. They also monitored the phones in the bars and restaurants they frequented.

Telephone tapping

Telephone tapping—the interception of spoken and electronic communications—is extensively used by the state in surveillance. In the UK there have been numerous cases in which it was revealed that the British intelligence services tapped the phones of social activists, labor unions, and civil liberties groups. However, while there are legitimate reasons for the police and other law enforcement agencies to be involved in telephone tapping, the technology is so easy to use that organized criminals, ruthless businesses, or obsessive individuals can tap telephones as easily as the police or government intelligence.

It is relatively easy to intercept a voice communication. Back in 1957, author and journalist Bob Keston was eager to demonstrate the threat to privacy posed by a simple phone-tapping mechanism.

It does not require a high level of skill or technology to intercept a voice communication. For example, the microphone in many older telephones may be replaced with one that can also transmit to a remote receiver. Taps may also be placed in telephone wiring systems in the basements of buildings, on the lines outside a house, or on the telephone poles near the target of surveillance.

System X

In the UK during the 1980s, British Telecom introduced System X—a digital technology designed to revolutionize the telephone system. It has the capacity to activate a line when the phone is in its cradle. The result is that most models of telephone start to transmit surrounding sounds. System X was designed as wiretap-friendly technology, allowing any line to be bugged from anywhere. This means that it is not just phone conversations that are tapped, but any conversation in the room. How much does it matter that the conversations of people who have no involvement in criminal or subversive activity are monitored?

Recent revelations in the UK magazine *Statewatch* indicate that a new worldwide arrangement has been made for the producers of telecommunications exchanges. The arrangement states that all exchanges must enable the interception of telecommunications. But what human rights violations might occur if a tyrannical regime suddenly has access to a national telephone tapping system?

New cellular phones use a digital system, which is more difficult to intercept than that of the old mobile phones and provides clearer conversations. It is also easier to secure these telephones from eavesdropping through scrambling. However, intelligence agencies in the United States and other countries have attempted to restrict the use of improved scrambling technology. In Pakistan,

James McCord, one of the main figures in the Watergate scandal of 1972, with a wiretapping device used to monitor the calls of President Richard Nixon's political opponents

the government shut down a cellular phone company until it provided equipment to allow easy over-the-air interception. In the United States, the cellular telephone industry agreed to adopt a weakened scrambling standard after pressure from the NSA. Experts who have seen the standard say that it provides almost no protection against eavesdropping. Intelligence agencies in other countries have also lobbied to limit the security feature in digital cellular phones.

Intelligence agencies believe that telephone tapping is essential to keeping tabs on terrorists, subversives, foreign agents, and the like. They therefore monitor mobile phones as extensively as they can with landlines. But civil liberties groups argue that individual citizens have the right to private telephone conversations. There is also the question of whether private telephone companies should act as an arm of government by not allowing scrambling devices on their phones.

Identity cards

Many people living around the world have to carry an identity (ID) card with them all the time. Originally these cards were introduced to ensure that enemies of the state would be forced either to register or exist without documents; then it would be easy for the police to pick them up. In some countries, like Spain, Portugal, Thailand, and Singapore, ID cards are becoming part of the government administration. Magnetic strips and microprocessor technology mean that they will be used to obtain welfare benefits and other services. This means that the government will be able to keep a closer eye on people's movements and activities. While, from the

A Wisconsin driver's license, which doubles as an ID card

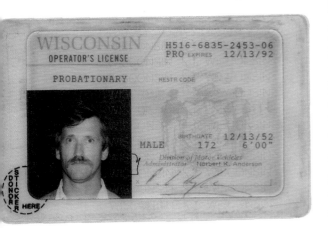

WISCONSIN
OPERATOR'S LICENSE
H516-6835-2453-06
PRO EXPIRES 12/13/92

PROBATIONARY   RESTR CODE

MALE   BIRTHDATE 12/13/52
172   6'00"
Division of Motor Vehicles
Administrator   Norbert K. Anderson

point of view of government, the security services and the police, it clearly makes sense to use ID cards more widely, many individuals might feel that the state—like George Orwell's Big Brother—knows too much about them.

Biometrics

Advances in technology are making another form of mass surveillance possible. Biometrics is the process of collecting, processing, and storing details of a person's physical characteristics for the purposes of identification and authentication. The most popular forms of biometric ID are retina scans, hand geometry, thumb scans, fingerprints, voice

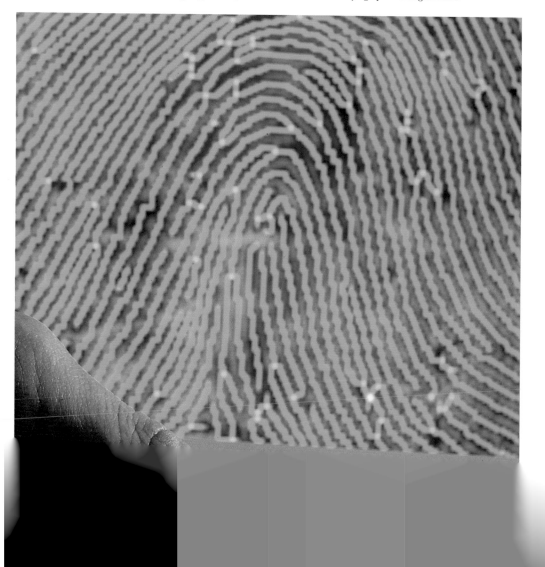

Biometric identification—a view of a fingerprint being scanned

recognition, and digitized (electronically stored) photographs. The technology has aroused the interest of governments and companies because, unlike other forms of ID such as cards or papers (which can be forged), it has the capacity to identify the target subject accurately and intimately.

Biometrics schemes are being implemented across the world. Spain has begun a national fingerprint system for unemployment benefits and health care entitlement. Russia has announced plans for a national electronic fingerprint system for banks. Jamaicans are required to scan their thumbs into a database before qualifying to vote at elections. In France and Germany, tests are underway with equipment that transfers fingerprint information onto credit cards. The technology is being used in shops, government agencies, child-care centers, and automated-teller machines.

An automated immigration system, developed by the U.S. Immigration and Naturalization Service, uses hand geometry. In this project, frequent travelers have their hand geometry stored in a smart computer chip card. The traveler places a hand on the scanner and the card into a slot. More than 70,000 people have enrolled in the trial. The plan may ultimately result in a worldwide identification system for travelers.

DNA identification
The most controversial form of biometrics, DNA identification, is benefiting from new scanning technology, which can automatically match DNA samples against a large database in minutes. Police forces in several countries, such as the United States, Germany, and Canada, are creating national databases of DNA. In the United Kingdom and the United States, when a particularly violent crime is committed, such as rape or murder, police may

demand that all individuals in a particular area should voluntarily provide samples or face being placed under scrutiny as a suspect.

Is DNA identification a marvelous invention or an invasion of privacy? The police say that widespread DNA testing would be a boon to crime-fighting. According to testimony before the U.S. National Commission on the Future of DNA Evidence, 30 percent of crime scenes have traces of semen, blood, or saliva, all of which contain human DNA. Do you agree with the argument that if we have nothing to hide, we should not have anything to be frightened of?

Critics of extensive DNA testing say that it can reveal a predisposition to hereditary disease and information that hints at traits like sexual orientation. What other uses could be made of DNA samples? Certainly insurance companies would be wary of insuring a person whose DNA pointed to a history of genetic disease.

A researcher examines DNA sequencing data. From this information it is possible to identify the unique DNA code of any individual.

Computers and the Internet

If computers are connected to any form of network —if they are part of an office network or if they use the Internet—they are likely to be subject to surveillance. Businesspeople carrying laptops have these routinely scanned when they enter the UK. Disks may be checked and encrypted files decoded. According to UK Customs and Excise: "So far as we are concerned, there is no difference between an encrypted file and a locked suitcase. All travelers entering the country should be prepared to have their equipment scanned." The routine scans are allegedly to locate illegal material, such as child pornography. Those who fail to cooperate may be arrested.

Over the past decade, the Internet has become an important tool for communication and research. The technology is growing phenomenally fast, with millions of users going on line each year. The

People using computers at an Internet café in Bonn, Germany. The police and government's interception of electronic mail messages for surveillance purposes has alarmed civil rights groups.

Internet is also used increasingly as a tool for buying and selling. The capability, speed, and reliability of the Internet are constantly improving, resulting in the continued development of new uses for the medium.

Police and governments have moved to intercept anything on the Internet, often using the search for child pornography as an excuse. They argue that the interception of e-mail traffic should be through agreements between police and Internet Service Providers (the channels for Internet traffic). This move has caused alarm, and civil rights groups have demanded that e-mail interception should not be treated any differently than telephone interception. In the UK, legislation passed in 2000 means that this is now the case. In Singapore, all Internet Service Providers are operated by government-controlled or related organizations. However, it may well be that any legislation governing the interception of e-mails has been passed too late.

Scrambling messages

Encryption has become the most important tool to protect against surveillance. With encryption, a message is scrambled so that only the intended recipient is able to unscramble, and subsequently read, the contents. The United States and UK governments have sought to limit encryption. Because terrorists and other criminals are likely to encode their communications, the UK government has argued that encryption is a national security risk. But the European Union was concerned that, if member governments could unscramble any messages, this would limit an individual's right to privacy and hinder plans to promote electronic commerce in Europe. The police and other law-enforcement agencies now have to obtain a warrant for decryption by the person concerned.

VIEWPOINTS

"In the past, technology has been the friend of the NSA, but in the last four or five years technology has moved from being the friend to being the enemy."
John Mills, ex-CIA officer and Head of Staff of the House of Representatives on the growth of antisurveillance technology

"[Encryption will] devastate our ability to fight crime and prevent terrorism."
Attorney General Janet Reno

FACT

Anonymous remailers strip identifying information from e-mails, and can stop traffic analysis. They are the Internet equivalent of P.O. Box addresses. The police and intelligence services are opposed to them. In Finland, a popular anonymous remailer had to be shut down because of legal challenges that forced the remailer to reveal the name of one of its users.

Encrypted computer information for protection against hackers

Future developments

During the twenty-first century, telecommunications will shift to high-capacity fiber-optic networks. These networks cannot be intercepted from a distance but require physical access; this will make it more difficult for foreign powers to tap them. For example, the United States will not be able to tap into such lines in Russia unless they can physically attach a bugging device. There will no longer be radio waves to intercept.

The United States government used to have a substantial lead in computers and information technology, but now their computers are the same standard as those used by leading industrial and academic organizations. The academic and industrial communities are using cryptography, which is a way of coding messages to keep them secure.

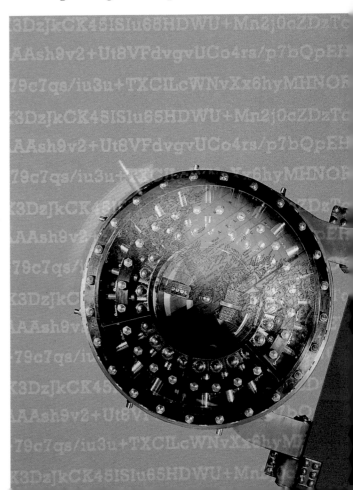

Some countries have freedom of information laws so that the citizens can find out much of what goes on in their name, but government surveillance is often specifically excluded from the list of things that people have a right to know. The problem with government surveillance is that we are told it must be confidential or else other countries will know all our secrets. But the big question for citizens of western democracies is—can we really trust our own governments?

The other question is the extent to which international power is linked to money. The United States has the resources to keep tabs on everybody else. The countries of Western Europe cannot match its resources and therefore lag behind in access to information. And developing countries are not even players in this international game. If knowledge is power, it seems that the countries with the most effective surveillance operations will win every time.

Surveillance technology is important to the operation of a nation's armed forces. In this 1996 photograph, Swedish sailors use surveillance equipment on the HMS Stromstad, a high-speed missile attack boat designed to thwart Russian amphibious attack ships in the Baltic.

DEBATE

Government surveillance is carried out in the name of the people and with public money. But the people do not know what is being monitored, or why, or how it is being monitored. Is it right that this should be the case?

POLICE SURVEILLANCE

Catching Criminals or Monitoring Minorities?

The police use a variety of surveillance methods both to catch criminals and to prevent crimes from being committed. Police surveillance needs to be covert, or hidden, so that criminals are not aware that they are being watched. The object of covert surveillance is to obtain information— either evidence or intelligence—that is impossible to obtain in any other way. Covert surveillance is often used alongside other policing methods, such as the use of informers and undercover police officers. Most forms of legal surveillance are justified as anticrime measures. But it needs to be asked whether, in many countries, the considerable powers afforded the police are sometimes abused.

The police are hard-pressed to keep track of white-collar criminals, who are involved in an ever-increasing range of activities. These Japanese suspects worked for the Hitachi Corporation, which was accused of spying on IBM.

The police are under constant pressure to keep up with the technological advances employed by criminals. White-collar criminals, so called because they are well educated and middle-class, are involved in an ever-increasing range of activities. These include information warfare, breaking copyright, international financial crime, national security threats, and Internet crime (such as charging for, but never supplying, products ordered over the Internet). With their advanced understanding of digital technology, these criminals are way ahead of the average police officer in these fields.

Because they have no criminal record, they are virtually invisible to conventional law enforcement; yet they control the fortunes of banks, corporations, and governments, moving huge amounts of money each day throughout hundreds of entities.

However, most police activity is focused on the more traditional crimes: from burglary to drug running. For these crimes, the police often use surveillance, without which there would undoubtedly be more organized and serious crime. The risk is that the same surveillance methods will increasingly be used on common offenses without public debate. The European Charter for Human Rights ensures that, in Europe, police forces are under scrutiny to comply with a recognized set of human rights standards. Bugging, using informers, and undercover officers are all accepted as part of a legal framework.

Criminal intelligence information has been described as the lifeblood of the modern police service. Information about known criminals, suspects, and their associates is gathered in various ways, but mainly through technical surveillance operations, closed-circuit television (CCTV) cameras, and informers. Indeed, much policing is aimed at gathering intelligence information rather than evidence. But the reliability and relevance of this intelligence information may vary.

VIEWPOINTS

"At the core of the debate is this conflict of interest between, on the one hand, the reasonable expectation of individuals to engage in private activities, including telephone conversations, without being overheard or recorded, and, on the other hand, the need to use sophisticated techniques to combat serious crime."
Madeleine Colvin of the UK organization Justice, 1998

"Undercover work offers a means of actively pursuing crime through direct involvement and police initiative. It fits with the notion of the modern police officer prevailing via intelligence, skill and finesse, rather than brute force and coercion."
Gary Marx, author of Undercover Work: A Necessary Evil

In drug-running cases, the police and army often use surveillance methods when working closely together. Here members of the Bolivian army burn illegally grown coca leaves. Coca is used to make cocaine.

Whereas criminal record information is based on hard facts, criminal intelligence is often speculative and difficult to verify. Even with CCTV, one might know where people are at a certain time, but not where they came from or where they are going. Certainly this sort of information has led to many successful convictions. However, during the course of surveillance, irrelevant information of a noncriminal nature will be collected about individuals and events.

There has been a political shift in targeting in recent years. Instead of investigating a crime after it happens, police forces are increasingly tracking the sort of people they think are most likely to commit a crime: certain social classes and races of people living in specific areas. This type of preemptive policing is called data-veillance and is based on the way in which the military gather huge quantities of low-grade intelligence for tactical purposes.

CCTV

In most industrial countries, CCTV cameras are just a normal part of modern life in towns and cities. Few people worry that they are being spied on; they are more likely to regard the cameras as a way of preventing crime. CCTV cameras operate by filming everything that appears in front of them. The images they record are normally displayed on a television screen or monitor. The screen can be watched all the time, like when a security guard uses CCTV to check what is happening outside a building. Sometimes the film is saved so that it can be looked at later, if necessary; for instance, to help identify the suspects in the case of a robbery.

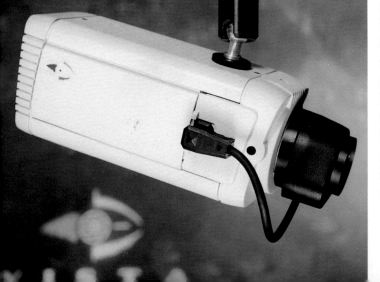

In many countries CCTV cameras, like the one below, are an accepted part of modern life.

CCTV technology has become increasingly sophisticated. Features include night vision, computer-assisted operation, and motion detection facilities, which allow the operator to instruct the system to switch on only when something moves in front of the camera. Some camera systems have bulletproof casing and automated self-defense mechanisms, so that it is very difficult to put them out of action.

Recent years have witnessed an explosion in the use of CCTV cameras. In some towns and cities, CCTV is seen to be as essential as the electricity supply or telephone network. It has become quite commonplace to find cameras placed in buses, trains, elevators, and even phone booths. Some people now expect to be filmed from the moment they leave their front door. Hidden cameras are installed in movie theaters, red-light districts, locker rooms, and on housing estates. Some police forces are considering fitting Minicams into police helmets and clothing.

This CCTV footage shows a man mugging a woman in the street.

A security guard with a bank of security monitors. Each screen shows a view of a shopping center taken from a different CCTV camera.

The UK leads the world in CCTV. There are more surveillance cameras per head than anywhere else. Up to $500 million a year is spent on CCTV, with about 95 percent of towns and cities installing CCTV equipment in town centers, shopping malls, parking garages, and on public transportation. About half a million low-budget CCTV kits have been sold, mostly to smaller store owners. In North America and Australia, cameras are increasingly being used to monitor public squares. In Singapore they are widely used to make drivers stick to speed limits and other rules and to prevent people from littering.

Many public buildings use CCTV cameras. In the United States, Utah's Salt Lake City district spent over $200,000 installing video surveillance cameras and recorders. The cameras scan parking lots and, in some cases, school hallways. They are not, however, used in bathrooms, showers, or other private areas. Many schools use them in parking lots to curb intrusions or fights among rival gangs.

With all this use of visual surveillance, there are remarkably few laws to protect the individual. The general attitude seems to be that you should not be in the wrong place at the wrong time. If you are a law-abiding citizen, CCTV can only protect you. Even Sweden, once strongly opposed to CCTV in public places, is considering relaxing its privacy laws. In Norway, filming by CCTV is legal, but there are restrictions on how the information is used. In the UK, data protection laws cover the film records obtained by CCTV, but there is no regulation about where the cameras are placed and how they are operated.

CCTV cameras are supposed to prevent crime and help people feel safer in public places. After all, the theory goes, not only will the cameras catch the criminals in the act, but also, if the criminals know that the cameras are there, they will be less likely to commit crimes. Therefore, the general public will feel safer when they see the CCTV cameras. Unfortunately, the research does not entirely support this theory. While a recent study claimed that CCTV was successful, two out of three studies into the effects of CCTV show that both crime and fear of crime have increased.

FACT

In Denmark, CCTV cameras are banned in public places.

A traffic sign warns drivers that they will be monitored by cameras measuring their speed.

There have undoubtedly been cases in which CCTV cameras have led to the arrest of criminals. In a famous British case, two boys abducted James Bulger, a two-year-old, from a Liverpool shopping mall and later killed him. The abduction was recorded on video by the CCTV cameras in the mall, and the boys were identified from their images on tape.

However, CCTV surveillance is also open to abuse. While cameras are sometimes installed in changing rooms and public toilets for security purposes, they are clearly an intrusion into an individual's privacy. In one case, a store owner had installed a video in his changing room and used it mainly to spy on female customers as they undressed. In Wales, a CCTV operator was convicted of more than two hundred obscenity charges after using cameras to spy on women and then making obscene calls to them from the control room.

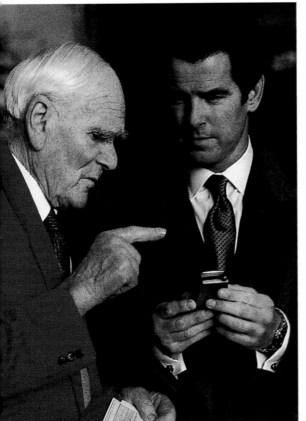

The character Q shows James Bond how to operate a miniaturized surveillance device hidden in a cigarette lighter in the movie Tomorrow Never Dies.

Secret visual surveillance

The art of visual surveillance has changed dramatically over recent years. Police and intelligence officers still photograph demonstrations and individuals of interest, but increasingly such images can be stored and searched. In Denmark, the police want to ban the use of masks by demonstrators so that it will be possible to identify every participant.

One of the major technological advances has been miniaturization, or making things much, much smaller. This means that cameras can be made so small that they are virtually undetectable. A technological development such as this opens up new possibilities of abuse by individuals, companies, and official agencies. Surveillance cameras for covert, or undercover, operations have been modified to the point where they are little more than a microchip and a pinhead lens. Cameras the size of a matchbox are commonplace.

Tiny cameras can be hidden in common household objects such as clocks and smoke alarms.

The future

New technology means that CCTV cameras are able to do far more than just record what goes on in front of them. It is now possible to program them to recognize certain individuals, turning CCTV from passive to active surveillance and targeting the movement of certain people in a particular area. This is known as algorithmic surveillance data analysis. Already a U.S. company called Software and Systems has piloted a system in London that can scan crowds and match faces against a database of images held in a remote computer. New algorithmic CCTV cameras can pick up the behavioral quirks of petty criminals and car thieves. Criminals approach the scene of a potential crime differently than noncriminals, and the camera can identify them and alert security staff that an offense is about to be committed.

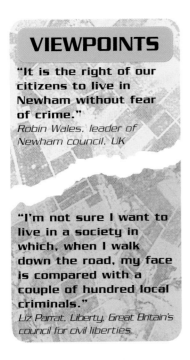

The linking of CCTV systems using facial recognition technology to databases holding photographs of individuals makes for a highly powerful surveillance tool. This technology has already been used at an English soccer stadium to help spot known troublemakers and at the Bank of Germany to restrict areas to authorized personnel only. In the London borough of Newham, CCTV cameras are programmed to recognize known criminals who visit the town center. So what kind of criminals are included on the register? How serious do their crimes need to be? How long ago have these crimes been committed? The police will not say who is on the database or how many offenders are included. All this is being done in the name of law and order, but individuals are being watched without any public debate about the -extent to which they should be watched.

In places where lots of people are gathered, CCTV has been used with facial recognition technology to spot troublemake

State-assisted telephone tapping

Police telephone tapping, or wiretapping, is conducted in nearly every country in the world. Although it has undoubtedly led to the arrest of many criminals, it has also been frequently abused. The U.S. State Department, in its annual Country Reports on Human Rights Practices for 1994, reported widespread illegal or uncontrolled use of wiretaps by governments and private groups in more than 70 countries. Are any of our calls private? Do we ever know that we are being, or have been, bugged—or who is bugging us? Should we have a right to know? Can we trust the police, or do we need a system that is less open to abuse?

Cordless telephones are becoming more and more popular in the West. In the United States alone, more than 40 million cordless phones are in use as well as millions of cellular phones. In Italy, there are more mobile phones than landline telephones. In developing countries, wireless communications such as cellular and satellite-based telephones are also popular as a means to avoid laying new telephone lines in areas that were previously undeveloped.

FACT

In the United States, wiretaps led to the conviction of 22,000 serious criminals between 1984 and 1994.

The signals from mobile phones can be intercepted using inexpensive scanners.

Signals from each of these devices—cordless telephones in particular—are easy to intercept. Many of the older models transmit just above the top range of the AM radio band, and conversations can easily be overheard with any AM radio. Newer models operate in the 49MHz range and can be intercepted with an inexpensive radio scanner available from many stores. The range of interception can be up to 1 mile (1.6 km).

FACT

Seventy percent of United States citizens think that all wiretaps should be banned.

This laptop computer is being used to intercept mobile phone calls. Its proximity to London's Houses of Parliament means that the user can listen in on MPs' phone conversations.

Cellular, or mobile, phones are also open to interception. They, too, broadcast over the airwaves like a radio. Inexpensive scanners are available to intercept conversations. More importantly, just using a mobile phone gives away its position and turns it into a tracking device. When a mobile phone is turned on, it regularly broadcasts its location to the local transmitters so that they can direct calls to the correct place. In an incident in Denmark, a murder trial was reopened against a member of the Hell's Angels because new evidence was found: Records from the telephone company proved that he had been near the scene of the crime when the murder took place.

Modern snoopers can buy specially adapted laptop computers and simply tune in to all the mobile phones active in the area by moving the cursor

down to the relevant phone number. The machine will even search for numbers to see if they are active.

Pagers

A pager, or beeper, is another electronic device that can be intercepted easily. Pagers receive signals over the airwaves with no scrambling. Computer programs are available that can monitor the entire frequency spectrum upon which pagers operate. Such programs can automatically retain every message that is sent.

In 1988, Congress passed a law allowing roving wiretaps. Before this law, each wiretap had to be approved by a judge, but now police can tap into any line they think might be used by, or is close to, a suspect. This means that if the police see someone they think might be a criminal entering your house or place of business, they can tap your phone without a warrant.

The police say that roving wiretaps will allow investigators to eavesdrop on criminals who are moving from phone to phone to avoid interception. But the law already permits this, provided it goes through a court. Many Americans believe that requiring the police to get the permission of a judge is essential to protect the privacy of the individual. More than 80 percent of calls intercepted by wiretap are innocent; roving wiretaps intercept an even higher percentage of calls placed by innocent parties who are not suspected of any crime.

While roving wiretaps are commonplace in the United States, there are no roving wiretaps in the UK, although one warrant (which gives permission) can include all the phone numbers of the person targeted. A Canadian report on wiretapping estimated that a single phone tap can affect up to 200 people.

FACT

British police conduct around 2,100 bugging operations a year. Mostly, officers enter premises and plant small, camouflaged transmitters. These pick up the conversations in a room and broadcast them to a listening station about 1.8 mi. (3 km) away. Since 1999 the police have had to apply for permission from a High Court judge to conduct most bugging operations.

New technology means that phone calls are now less likely to be tapped. But in Europe and the United States, legislation has been introduced that forces the telephone companies to build in a facility for police bugging.

The 1994 Communications Assistance in Law Enforcement Act (CALEA) gave the Federal Bureau of Investigation (FBI) extraordinary powers to demand that telephone companies restructure their networks to make wiretapping easier. Until 1994 the police had had to find the correct copper wire to tap into. Now telephone exchanges have to be designed so that lines can be tapped. Manufacturers must work with industry and law-enforcement officials to ensure that their equipment meets federal standards. A court can fine a company $10,000 a day for each product that does not comply.

The EU-FBI Surveillance System

European police forces have laid the foundations for a massive eavesdropping system capable of intercepting all mobile phone calls, Internet communications, fax, and pager messages. This is part of a strategy to create a seamless web of telecommunications surveillance across national boundaries. The move to establish the system follows a five-year lobbying exercise by agencies like the FBI. The plans for this surveillance program, known as the EU-FBI Surveillance System, were laid in secret. All Internet Service Providers (ISPs) will have to provide agencies with complete access to communications, regardless of country of origin.

The 1998 movie Enemy of the State *involves a lawyer (Will Smith, left) who is hunted by the NSA using all the surveillance technology at their disposal. An advertising campaign for the film read: "It's not paranoia if they're really out to get you...."*

This system will be capable of tracking suspects wherever they travel by means of subject tagging. Known as the International User Requirements for Interception (IUR), the tagging system will create a data processing and transmission network. This network will have details of the names, addresses, and phone numbers of targets and associates; it will also have their e-mail addresses, credit card details, PINs (personal identification numbers), and passwords.

It is reasonable to expect police forces from different countries to work together to stop crime. Terrorists and organized criminals travel easily from one country to another, especially in Europe with its lax border controls, so a global interception system must be a positive development. But some people are concerned that the EU-FBI Surveillance System was conceived in secret, with no democratic scrutiny.

Anyone using a cash card may find that his or her transaction is tracked.

FACT

In the United States, courts show that federal electronic intercepts have increased by up to 40 percent since President Bill Clinton took office in 1992. No federal magistrate has turned down a federal request for an intercept order since 1988.

Call analysis

In 1992, a group of senior law-enforcement officers met at FBI headquarters in Washington, D.C., to devise a strategy for dealing with environmental activists. The group hit on a plan that has become increasingly popular among police forces throughout the world. The FBI subpenaed (gave official written orders to supply documentation) 600 leading environmental activists regarding their telephone billing information. To most people, the information on a telephone bill is relatively unimportant: a few numbers, times, and dates. But to the FBI, it was a goldmine. By combining the calling information of all known activists, the authorities were able to build a vast tree involving tens of thousands of environmentalists. They could tell who worked with whom. They knew how the networks were formed and how they communicated. In a nutshell, the FBI was able to expose the

The security services are able to compile "friendship networks" of groups they suspect; environmentalists, like these people demonstrating below, come into this cateogory.

intimate details of all the interrelationships within the environmental movement. The environmental strategy was not unique. That year, the phone records of more than a million people in the United States were subpenaed by law-enforcement agencies.

In the United Kingdom this is called metering, and the police do not even need a warrant for it. The European Court of Human Rights ruled more than a decade ago that the practice, unless it was properly regulated, violated the European Convention on Human Rights, but the number of operations has grown steadily. In 1997, it was fifteen times more prevalent than phone tapping.

Most police forces in the UK are now using call analysis programs that are many times more powerful than those used by the U.S. authorities. The WatCall and Watson systems, produced by the Cambridge company Harlequin Intelligence Systems, can collect, collate, and analyze information on any fax or telephone call made in the UK. Called numbers are identified by subscriber name and address, and this mass of data is then merged with information from powerful police intelligence systems such as HOLMES. Police can use the WatCall system to secure details of your network of friends, which they then combine with intelligence data in HOLMES and finally build a comprehensive profile of your friends and family via the Watson intelligence system.

Once again, the question surrounding this issue is mainly about safeguards. Who is being targeted? Is there a difference between an ecoterrorist who has no respect for the law and a concerned environmentalist who organizes demonstrations to get the law changed? Should the activities of both be monitored in the same way?

FACT

In 1993, the multinational giant Procter & Gamble persuaded a judge to order the seizure of the telephone records of the long-distance calls of virtually the entire population of Cincinnati, Ohio. The aim? To trace the person who had been leaking confidential business information to the *Wall Street Journal*. The authorities secured 35 million records from 850,000 homes, but failed to pinpoint the source of the leaks.

The talon system, above, recognizes vehicle license plates and can be used to track a car around a city.

Traffic

Vehicle recognition systems have been developed that can identify a car's license plate and then track the car around a city using a computerized geographic information system. Systems such as the talon system, introduced in 1994 by UK company Racal, are now commercially available. This system is designed to recognize license plates and works during the day and at night. Initially it was used for traffic monitoring, but its function has been adapted in recent years to cover security surveillance. It has been incorporated in the "ring of steel," a series of roadblocks set up around the financial district of London after an Irish Republican Army bomb attack. The system can record all the vehicles that entered or left the district on any particular day.

Surveillance systems such as this raise significant issues of accountability, particularly when they are used by authoritarian regimes. The cameras used in Tiananmen Square in Beijing, China, were sold as advanced traffic systems. Yet they recorded the demonstrations by students in 1989. After the Chinese military had crushed the demonstrations, images of suspected subversives were repeatedly broadcast on Chinese television with the offer of a reward for information about them.

Foreign companies are exporting traffic control systems to Lhasa in Tibet, but Lhasa does not as yet have any traffic control problems. Foreign observers believe that the Chinese government, which occupies the country, is using them to spy on radicals.

New technology is not only available to investigators, but also to those engaging in criminal activity, particularly those involved in serious and organized crime. The race to stay ahead of the game is one reason why the technology is developing fast. But another reason is that the manufacturers of such technologies are eager to advance their businesses in new markets, with new demands.

DEBATE

Do law-abiding citizens need to fear telephone tapping and CCTV if the technologies used target criminals and help to make the world a safer place?

In 1989, surveillance cameras in Tiananmen Square, China, recorded the faces of students protesting against the Chinese government.

CORPORATE SURVEILLANCE

Customer Convenience or the Big Sell?

A hundred years ago, the way in which a business attracted customers was very different to the way it does so today. Then, a manufacturing company would simply advertise its wares on a billboard or in a newspaper. Today, businesses want to know a lot about us. They want to target the people who are most likely to buy their goods and services. Every time we use a credit card or store card or buy something on the Internet, the transaction is noted, not just to ensure that we pay our bills but to mark what sort of goods we buy, what are our interests, and what prices we are prepared to pay.

Every time we pay for goods by credit card, the transaction is noted.

There is now electronic market surveillance—the gathering of information such as itemized phone bills, credit card exchanges, and bank withdrawals. This basic commercial surveillance has been going on for decades, but new technology means that information can be collected and collated more effectively. So, in modern life do we have to accept that nothing is private? Should we have a right to know what information is being held on us and by whom?

Many of us do not realize just how much of our personal information is kept on file. In the West, most adults have a credit rating based on a mass of personal and financial information. These confidential details include the size of a person's income and mortgage, how many credit cards he or she owns, and whether he or she is in debt. The person concerned will not have supplied much of the information, and some of it may even be inaccurate, but it will affect his or her ability to borrow money and to buy anything on credit.

A whole host of agencies hold personal information about us, from health records to driving license details. We probably assume that this information is handled with complete confidentiality—but, in some instances, we would be wrong. In many countries, the government, the police, or even commercial interests often have access to that information. But we do not know what information is being held about us and, in some countries, would not even have the right to find out.

The information we part with when using a discount card may be very useful for commercial surveillance.

VIEWPOINTS

"[They have] the potential to become Big Brother's little helper."
Roland Moreno, the inventor of smart cards, on his creation

"Going from magnetic strip cards to chip cards is like going from a horse and buggy to a space shuttle. In doing so, we will make it possible for people to carry computers in their pockets."
Robert Selander, Chief Executive of MasterCard

The senior vice president of MasterCard International displays "the most advanced smart card in existence" at its launch in Sydney, Australia.

Smart cards

Smart cards are credit-card-sized microprocessors, which can be programmed to perform many different tasks. Australia leads the way in smart card technology, because smart card promoters have tested and launched their products there. At the moment most smart cards are used like credit cards, but instead of having the money debited from his or her account, the user pays for the card in advance. The card stores electronic money, which can be used for small transactions like telephone calls and travel on public transportation. Smart cards are also used in closed societies such as university campuses for purchases in stores and restaurants.

These cards represent the first step in a move toward a cashless society. Smart cards are fundamentally different from cash in that purchases are no longer anonymous. The business that the smart card holder is buying from can make a record of the date, time, and location of all transactions. It will also monitor the details of goods purchased, telephone use, car parking, attendance at the movies, and any other activities paid for by the smart card. These records will be processed and stored in central databases, where they will be used to create detailed customer profiles.

The organizations that are selling smart cards to the stores are actively marketing the development of these customer profiles. For example, in Visa's promotional material, one proposed application involves a terminal that can read a microchip's memory to identify a cardholder's specific interests and/or buying preferences. Is it enough to know that every transaction on a smart card is recorded and filed? Should we have any say over what happens to that information, and to whom it is given?

Privacy and the Internet

The recording of information about specific Internet activities has become one of the biggest emerging threats to Internet privacy. Every time a user accesses a Web page, the server holding the page logs the user's Internet address along with the time and date.

Some websites place "cookies" on users' machines. Cookies are programs designed to track people's activities at a detailed level. Other sites ask for the user's name, address, and other personal details before allowing access. Internet purchases are similarly recorded. On-line stores value such data very highly, not least for the potential to sell it to marketers and other organizations.

Purchases over the Internet are recorded, and the information may be sold to other organizations.

Triangulating data

Data from different sources can be put together on computer to compile detailed personal profiles. Triangulating data—the restoration of identification to supposedly anonymous data—can be produced by accessing the information stored on many different databases. Latanya Sweeney, an American academic based in Massachusetts, had access to the health data of state employees and their families. The names and addresses of these people had been removed to make the information anonymous, and the database had been sold to researchers for pharmaceutical companies and to a couple of universities.

For $20, Sweeney bought two floppy disks containing the voting register for Cambridge, Massachusetts. She integrated these disks with the supposedly anonymous medical information. The birth date alone was sufficient to identify 12 percent of the population; birth date and gender gave her the names and addresses of another 29 percent. With only four elements, she was able to identify 97 percent of the data. So, with the help of a computer, the pharmaceutical companies effectively had bought the health records of state employees and could identify the individuals.

Sweeney's actions show how personal information, including sensitive details like medical records, can be gathered by commercial companies without breaking the law. Should we be able to keep private companies from getting hold of our data?

Photograph of Latanya Sweeney, taken from her website. By integrating information from different databases, Sweeney proved that it was possible for companies to compile detailed personal profiles of most of the population.

Commercial satellites

As far as most people know, commercial satellites cannot eavesdrop on e-mails, faxes, or telephone calls. Their spying is purely visual. However, the technology is improving at such a rate that little is private from these detectors orbiting the Earth.

In 1988, a Russian commercial satellite relayed to Earth pictures of such clarity that they were detailed enough to distinguish objects as small as a car or a garden shed. A viewer would be able to pick out a house within a neighborhood, or examine potential building sites. The price of downloading these images was between $9.00 and $25. The satellite collected pictures of the southeastern United States, from Mississippi eastward, and from the tip of Florida to Washington, D.C.

However, a mere eleven years later, a commercial satellite capable of distinguishing objects the size of a tray was launched in the United States. The *Ikonos-1* is the most powerful commercial imaging satellite yet built. Its parabolic lens can record pictures of objects down to a size of 30 in. (80 cm) long anywhere on Earth. It is the first of a new generation of high-

FACT

In 1996, Aaron Nabil legally obtained a copy of the Oregon license plate database by paying $222. He then put the database on the Worldwide Web so that anyone could look up drivers' personal details. After a public uproar, he scrapped his site.

This commercial satellite image of Washington, D.C., shows the White House in the center-top and the largest office building in the world, the Pentagon, on the far left.

resolution satellites that use technology formerly restricted to government security agencies. Another ten companies have received licenses to launch equally powerful satellites.

Since the end of the Cold War, companies such as Earthwatch, Motorola, and Boeing have invested billions of dollars in the creation of satellites that are capable of mapping the most minute detail on the face of the Earth. The technology is already being used for a vast range of purposes, from media reporting of war and natural disasters, to detecting unlicensed building work and even illegal swimming pools. If we are out-of-doors, our movements can be recorded. There is nothing to prevent the pictures from being taken but, in countries with data protection legislation, there are laws preventing the use of photographs with people in them.

This image from the Ikonos satellite shows the streets of New York City with startling clarity.

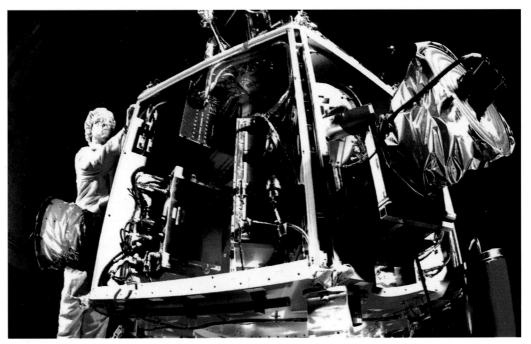

Technicians at work on the Ikonos *satellite*

European privacy legislation

There is a great divide between the United States and Europe on whether personal information should be passed on for commercial gain. The European Data Protection Directive, which was passed in 1995 but only came into effect at the end of the decade, makes every country in Europe conform to a common set of standards. These bind all governments and corporations to a rigorous observance of privacy. Article 25 forbids companies from exporting personal information on European citizens to other companies or countries that do not have adequate privacy protection.

This directive has angered the United States. Any organization, or country, that cannot protect privacy will be prohibited from conducting trade with Europe. The new rules will especially affect banks, travel and leisure companies, credit-card companies, Internet commerce companies, and multinationals, all of which move vast amounts of personal data around the globe.

In 1988, Anitha Bondestam, Sweden's privacy watchdog organization, acted to protect Swedish citizens whose details were being collected routinely at point of booking for flights to the United States. The organization instructed American Airlines to delete all health and medical details on Swedish citizens unless their explicit consent was obtained.

The law allows the export of data from Europe only under certain conditions. In most cases, there must be unambiguous consent before a company or agency can process data relating to the public. And the processing of sensitive personal information (religion, sexual preference, etc.) will be prohibited without explicit consent. Importantly, a data processor cannot use data for any other purpose than the one for which it was originally intended. So, if you give your personal details to a supermarket for the purpose of obtaining a reward card, the supermarket cannot use that data to check out your financial status. Or if you register to enter a website, the company cannot sell that information to a direct marketing company. Such practices are commonplace in North America, and the privacy commissioners of most European countries find this unacceptable.

The Data Protection Directive has sounded a warning to everyone doing business with Europe. It entitles European citizens to demand that any international company doing business with Europe meets European standards on privacy. This gives citizens some protection against personal information being handed out, but, if trade with the United States is at stake, how rigidly are the Europeans going to stick to the directive?

Relaxing outside a café in Amsterdam, Holland—but how much privacy do these European citizens have, and how much privacy do they have a right to?

Employee surveillance

Most businesses offering telemarketing services monitor their staff when they are dealing with customers by telephone for training and quality control purposes. The telephone caller is usually alerted to the fact that this is happening. But businesses are also using technology to keep an eye on their employees to make sure that they are working properly. At one American workplace, office workers were notified by management that they were not to conduct personal business on company time. A few weeks later, several workers were given written warnings—the evidence against them consisted of e-mail letters that had been taken from their personal, interoffice e-mail accounts. In a 1993 survey of large American corporations, 22 percent admitted they spied on their workers with some form of electronic surveillance and never told the workers that they were being monitored.

In the United States in particular, more and more employers are using CCTV to spy on their workers. While the companies say that such surveillance is justified—to make sure that workers are not wasting company time—many would question aspects of it, especially when it is aimed at intimidating people and discouraging them from union activities. Following some organizing activity by a local union, one U.S. employer installed video cameras to monitor each individual workstation and worker. Although the employer said that the technology was being used solely for safety monitoring, two employees were suspended for leaving their

> **FACT**
>
> In the United States in 1990, about eight million workers were subject to some form of electronic surveillance by their employers. By 1996, the number had risen to twenty million.

> **VIEWPOINT**
>
> "Desktop Surveillance offers a unique approach to the problem of access control, prevention of, or misuse of, computer equipment and software. It is the software equivalent of a surveillance camera."
> *Internet advertisement aimed at company bosses who want to monitor the behavior of their workers*

Telemarketing staff are monitored for training and quality control purposes.

DEBATE

What rights should people have to privacy at work? Should they have a right to conduct private business? Should employers be entitled to monitor their workforce all the time just because they pay their salary?

The use of video cameras to watch employees is on the increase. Are surveillance cameras replacing human supervisors at work? Does being filmed make for a happy working environment?

workstations to visit the restroom without permission. According to a 1993 report of the International Labor Office, the activities of some union representatives were inhibited by the reticence of other workers who knew that their conversations were being monitored.

In another American case, factory workers noticed a crew of outside electricians installing an extraordinary amount of new electric exit signs and refurbishing old ones. On examination, they found that each exit sign had been installed with a miniature video camera to watch the workers. In the United Kingdom and the United States, there are few legal constraints on video surveillance, unlike in Austria, Germany, Norway, and Sweden, where the law obligates employers to seek agreement with workers on such matters.

PROTECTING THE CITIZEN

The Right to Privacy or the Right to Pry?

In the twenty-first century, advances in technology mean that even more is known about us—what we do, where we go, to whom we speak, and what we say. Surveillance and antisurveillance technologies are now being sold in many stores, as well as via the Internet. With the development of ever more sophisticated equipment, the price of existing technologies will come down, bringing them within the range not only of police and national security agencies but also of private investigators and the media. As we become more vulnerable to all sorts of secret surveillance, it seems logical to suggest that we need to be protected by the law. The European Union is developing comprehensive privacy legislation, but how effective will this be, and how far will it affect surveillance by private bodies?

Surveillance legislation

Various arguments are made against the introduction of surveillance legislation. There is the argument that says protecting the innocent also protects the guilty—and what do the innocent have to fear from surveillance? There is the argument that says businesses need more information to target their sales accurately—and, after all, the people targeted by business are not forced to make purchases, so who does this really harm? There is the argument that says government departments need to gather more information about their citizens to ensure the accuracy of their long-term plans and forecasts. But what about a

FACT

Nearly 50 countries have laws on privacy and data protection or are in the process of passing such laws.

citizen's right to privacy, and how is that right balanced against the need for security of the state?

In George Orwell's *1984*, Big Brother was capable of spying on anyone at any time, so no one felt safe to say or do anything subversive. While, technically, our every move and word could be under surveillance, in fact, the sheer cost of mounting such an operation means that this is unlikely to happen. Surveillance always has to be targeted. However, our governments and police forces certainly have the potential to exercise considerable powers. While civilian surveillance is targeted, military surveillance uses a trawling technique that gathers up information about the innocent as well as the guilty.

A "spy plane" used by the armed forces for surveillance and reconnaissance

What is a legitimate surveillance target? A person known to be involved in organized crime? A suspected pedophile? A neo-Nazi group? Does the process of legally tracking a person or group provide a license for indiscriminate mass targeting? Many surveillance operations—the Echelon system, for example—go beyond the limits of the law. While his nightmare vision of Big Brother may not have come about, many of the technologies used for surveillance today would have been beyond Orwell's wildest dreams.

There is, however, a huge difference between the need of governments and law-enforcement agencies to keep the state secure and apprehend criminals and the commercial needs of business. Private companies use surveillance to target customers more effectively and to stay ahead of the competition. Should the government ensure that legislation exists to prevent confidential personal records from falling into the hands of private businesses? While the development of new surveillance technologies is set only to continue, the situation regarding people's individual rights and freedoms requires close and careful monitoring.

DEBATE

Do we need an independent watchdog in every country to protect the privacy of individuals from surveillance?

*Communications antennas in Phoenix, Arizona. Who's listening to **your** phone calls?*

GLOSSARY

arms deals business activities involving the buying and selling of weapons

bugging device a hidden microphone used for recording conversations

CIA Central Intelligence Agency; a U.S. bureau that conducts espionage and intelligence activities

civil liberty the right of an individual to certain freedoms of speech and action

Cold War the state of political hostility and military tension that occurred between the United States and the Soviet Union following World War II

communist a supporter of a classless society in which private ownership has been abolished and the means of production and subsistence belong to the community

decryption the decoding of an encrypted message

democracy government by the people or their elected representatives

encryption the coding of a message so that it cannot be understood

espionage the act or practice of spying

global power struggle the fight between certain countries to be rich and influential

intelligence information found out by covert means; for example, by spying

intercept to stop or seize on the way from one place to another

internment the act of detaining enemy citizens during wartime

landline a telecommunications wire or cable laid over land

legislation government laws

money laundering the act of processing money acquired illegally to make it appear that it has been acquired legally

organized crime an enterprise involving a number of people, whose purpose is to gain profit and power from illegal activities

radical favoring ideas or actions that are different from those generally accepted

status quo the way things are

subversive a person who tries to undermine the government

telex a printed message sent by telephone

totalitarian regime a system of government where all activities are controlled by an unelected leader

transition the change from one state or stage to another

BOOKS TO READ

Day, Dwayne A, ed. *Eye in the Sky: The Story of the Corona Spy Satellites*. Smithsonian Institution Press, 1998.

Decew, Judith Wagner. *In Pursuit of Privacy: Law, Ethics, and the Rise of Technology*. Cornell University Press, 1997.

Larsen, Tom. *The Layman's Guide to Electronic Eavesdropping: How It's Done and Simple Ways to Prevent It*. Paladin Press, 1996.

Orwell, George. *1984*. New American Library Classics, 1990 reissue.

Staples, William G. *The Culture of Surveillance: Discipline and Social Control in the United States*. St. Martin's Press, 1997.

Whitaker, Reg. *The End of Privacy: How Total Surveillance Is Becoming a Reality*. New Press, 1999.

USEFUL ADDRESSES

United States

American Civil Liberties Union
125 Broad Street
18th Floor
New York, NY 10004-2400
http://www.aclu.org

Electronic Privacy and Information Center
666 Pennsylvania Avenue SE
Suite 301
Washington, DC 20003
http://www.epic.org

Federal Trade Commission
600 Pennsylvania Avenue, N.W.
Washington, DC 20580
http://www.ftc.org

Privacy International Washington Office
666 Pennsylvania Avenue, SE
Suite 301
Washington, DC 20003
http://www.privacy.org/pi/

Canada

**Information and Privacy
Commissioner Ontario**
80 Bloor Street West
Suite 1700
Toronto
Ontario M5S 2V1
http://www.ipc.on.ca

INDEX

INDEX